COACHED
BY
JOSEMARÍA, ESCRIVÁ

COACHED BY JOSEMARÍA ESCRIVÁ

Lessons in Discipleship

FR. JOHN HENRY HANSON, O. PRAEM.

 Scepter

Published by Scepter Publishers, Inc.
info@scepterpublishers.org
www.scepterpublishers.org
800-322-8773
New York
All rights reserved.

Cover art: St. Josemaría Escrivá, protected by copyright © Prelature of the Holy Cross and Opus Dei, and used with permission.
Cover design: Studio Red Design
Text design and pagination: Studio Red Design
All images of St. Josemaría Escrivá in this book are protected by copyright © Prelature of the Holy Cross and Opus Dei, and used with permission.

Library of Congress Control Number: 2023940572

ISBN Print: 978-1-59417-508-4
eBook: 978-1-59417-509-1

Printed in the United States of America

Contents

Introduction: Speaking Confidentially 1

One: Is It All about Work? 9

Two: What Work Is All About 19

Three: Rest, Recreation, & Renewal:
Luxury or Duty? 29

Four: Not for Your Coffee Mug:
The Unquotable St. Josemaría 41

Five: Clay Made Divine: Material for Sanctity...........51

Six: Strong Language: The Tough Talk We Need 59

Seven: Even Stronger Language:
The Encouragement We Need........................73

Eight: Struggle & Perseverance 81

Nine: "What Are You Waiting For?" 95

I have noticed at times how an athlete's eyes light up at the sight of the obstacles he has to overcome. What a victory there is in store! See how he conquers the difficulties! God Our Lord looks at us that way. He loves our struggle: we will win through always, because he will never deny us his all-powerful grace. Thus, it doesn't matter if we have to fight, because he does not abandon us.

—St. Josemaría Escrivá, *Friends of God*, no. 182

Introduction

Speaking Confidentially

Let me continue, as I have always done, to speak to you confidentially.[1]

If you have read Alexandre Havard's first book in Scepter's *Coached by* series, you heard St. Joan of Arc speak—and speak directly to you. Havard imaginatively (but plausibly) makes her speak as a "coach," in keeping with what she did in real life: she was a military commander, an inspiration for her nation, and catalyst for her troops. Her story is so well known and, by secular standards, simply anomalous and inexplicable. Or, if secular historians do try to make sense of her apart from the Catholic Faith, they misconstrue her obedience to God as rebellion against the order

---

1. Josemaría Escrivá, *Furrow* (New York: Scepter, 2002), no. 238.

established by God in male and female relationships and the roles which nature assigns to each sex.

The main point, however, is not what the world makes of her, but what God made of her. Saints, empowered by God's grace, can do just about anything—indeed, "all things in him," as St. Paul attests (Phil 4:13). The weak and poor of the world shame the powerful and rich, and this has been true since God, way back in Genesis, first started calling individuals to do great and difficult things in his name. Those who have faith marvel at St. Joan of Arc, but we don't write her off as an historical fluke—as though she just happened to be in the right place at the right time, and impersonal forces randomly converged to make her mission possible. Her story has God's fingerprints all over it.

Havard makes this maiden speak to us. He takes her personality and deeds from a remote century and makes them relatable, comprehensible to us who live over six hundred years later. He lets Joan direct and instruct us by breaking down her accomplishments into grace and virtues—not happenstance or magic, but trust in God and virtuous living.

With St. Josemaría Escrivá (1902–1975), no such imaginary monologues or pep talks need be dreamt up. He has left us with not only a substantial collection of written works, but also numerous hours of video footage.

Many of his talks and dialogues in Opus Dei get-togethers (convened in small groups or among hundreds, sometimes thousands) are recorded for us, revealing the personality, tone of voice, mannerisms, and spirit of the man who founded The Work of God.

He considered these meetings as family style gatherings, and so they were characterized by a casual and familiar atmosphere. Even the platform from which he spoke was often decorated to resemble a domestic living room.

Why this is important to mention in a book like this is that he already considered his relationship to his spiritual children to be both fatherly and directive—qualities of a good coach. He was coaching all the time, but in a paternal and natural way, the way wisdom and guidance would be shared in a living room among a close-knit family.

You can't miss it in his writings either. Directive words such as "look," "listen," "you can," and many others show a man forcefully conducting his listeners to a goal. Only someone who knows the goal, preferably by experience, may be relied upon to show the way to it. The old saying, "Those who can, do; those who cannot, teach,"[2] might be true for some, but for spiritual masters, it really can't be. One can teach spiritual "theory" all day, and teach it

---

2. Normally attributed to George Bernard Shaw, from his play *Man and Superman* (1905), where the line is: "He who can, does. He who cannot, teaches."

accurately. But our Lord seems to place more value on imitation than book knowledge, as when he condemns the Pharisees for not doing what they teach, and for arrogating to themselves spiritual titles such as "Teacher" and "Father," which only the experienced truly deserve.

St. Josemaría's introductory remarks to his classic *The Way* sets a familial tone not only for his counsels but for the contents of this book. He is both extremely gentle and insistent:

> Read these counsels slowly. Pause to meditate their meaning. They are things that I whisper in your ear, as a friend, as a brother, as a father. We shall speak intimately; and God will be listening to us. I am going to tell you nothing new. I shall only stir your memory so that some thought may arise and strike you: and so your life will improve and you will set out along the way of prayer and of Love. And in the end you will become a soul of worth.[3]

From all the personal advice St. Josemaría addresses to his readers in books such as *The Way*, *Furrow*, and *The Forge*, this book will attempt to distill and reflect on certain of the saint's counsels aimed at disciples and discipleship. In his writings and talks, he addresses leaders, souls of prayer, parents, students, many different types of people,

---

3. Josemaría Escrivá, *The Way* (New York: Scepter, 2002), author's preface.

and many aspects of Christian life. Our focus here is to glean lessons in discipleship from one who considered himself just that, a disciple, before anything else he later became. He never wanted people to call him the founder of anything; he objected that the work he did was God's, and all he did was get in the way!

A final point. It is difficult in a book like this to avoid stringing together quotations and commentary. One is always better advised to go straight to the source and simply read St. Josemaría himself. Yet it is my hope that by introducing the unacquainted reader with the saint, that the selections will stimulate such deeper reading of Escrivá's works. You have to start somewhere, and if this is your somewhere, welcome to it. It is my privilege to be your guide, even your coach, at the starting line.

To readers already veterans in the ranks of this zealous coach, perhaps this unique culling of his teachings will stimulate a fresh fire in the soul. Looking at something familiar through a new prism can reveal facets previously unnoticed and, therefore, unappreciated and unapplied to one's life.

Let us begin with a word of his prayerful encouragement:

Speak now from the bottom of your heart: "Lord, I really do want to be a saint. I really do want to be a worthy disciple of yours and to follow you unconditionally." And now you should make a resolution to renew each day the great ideals which inspire you at this moment.

Oh, Jesus, if only we who are united in your Love were truly persevering! If only we could translate into deeds the yearnings you yourself awaken in our souls! Ask yourselves often, "What am I here on earth for?" It will help you in your efforts to finish all your daily tasks perfectly and lovingly, taking care of the little details. Let us turn to the example of the saints. They were people like us, of flesh and bone, with failings and weaknesses, who managed to conquer and master themselves for love of God. Let us consider their lives and, like bees who distil precious nectar from each flower, we shall learn from their struggles.[4]

---

4. Josemaría Escrivá, *Friends of God* (New York: Scepter, 2002), no. 20.

One

Is It All about Work?

The strange thing would be not to talk to God, to draw away and forget him, and busy ourselves in activities which are closed to the constant promptings of his grace.[5]

We associate coaching with sports: organized effort, drills, running plays, strategy, winning.

Applied to other areas of life, coaching makes us think of motivation to get things done, to persevere, to push through to a goal. A personal trainer keeps an athlete from using bad form in working out while also driving him to increase weight or tension and reps. It depends on what the exercise is for: bulking up, endurance, or both.

---

5. Escrivá, *Friends of God*, no. 251.

In nonathletic areas of life, a coach might assume the role of a Twelve Step sponsor, an accountability partner, a dieting buddy, or a mentor. In each case, we are looking to another person to keep us on the right path and motivate us when we slip. Likewise in each case, we are looking for someone to get us to do something hard that, left to ourselves, we would probably avoid or do badly.

Does the spiritual life fit into this mode of thinking? In fact, having leaders and guides is a part of the divine structure of the Church. The image of the shepherd, of bishops and presbyters, assumes flocks and assemblies of people who need instruction, motivation, correction, and the like. The Old Testament employs shepherd imagery in prophesying the Messiah, and Jesus himself identifies his mission as a quintessentially pastoral one:

> I am the good shepherd; I know my own and my own know me, . . . and I lay down my life for the sheep. And I have other sheep, that are not of this fold; I must bring them also, and they will heed my voice. So there shall be one flock, one shepherd. (Jn 10:14–16)

From New Testament times, to the monks of the Egyptian desert, to religious communities of consecrated life, to lay movements in the Church, to individuals seeking spiritual direction from their parish priest—each assumes not only a hierarchy, but a system of personal accountability overseen by one who has the spiritual care of his respective flock.

But although the Church employs "coaches" in her very structure, the comparison fails if we think exclusively of doing something and/or winning something. Christian coaching goes much deeper than executing drills and winning games.

That deeper place is the soul—God's country, in other words. Its dispositions, purity, moral character, prayerfulness—all of these matter more to God than whatever heap of good works we can amass from dawn to dusk. Christian coaching cannot bypass the inner self for the sake of busying the outer self with activity. Christians looking for something to do will find in a good coach someone who first wants to know who they are. They will want to find out where both heart and treasure call home, what the individual considers the most important thing about himself.

A simple chapter like this forestalls any expectation that you are reading a series of chapters featuring St. Josemaría telling you how to do spiritual stuff. Yes, you should have the Mass at the center of your life and the rosary never far from your fingers. You know these things already. What may not be as obvious to us are the effects such things should be producing in us—the gospel fruits which our Lord says come directly (and *exclusively*) from our union with him (see Jn 15:1–8).

Here is what the saint actually says about action devoid of soul:

> A friend of mine was dreaming once. . . . He was flying very high, but he was not inside the plane, in the cabin. He was outside, on the wings. Poor soul, how he suffered! What anguish! It was as if Our Lord was showing him that just such insecurity and danger faces apostolic souls who would fly up to the heights of God, but have no interior life, or else neglect it. They are full of anxiety and doubt, and in constant danger of coming to grief.
>
> I really do believe that a serious danger of losing the way threatens those who launch out into action—activism!—while neglecting prayer, self-denial and those means without which it is impossible to achieve a solid piety: receiving the Sacraments frequently, meditation, examination of conscience, spiritual reading and constant recourse to Our Lady and the Guardian Angels. . . . Besides, all these means contribute in a way that nothing else can to making the Christian's daily life a joyful one, for, from their hidden riches, flow out the sweetness and joy of God, like honey from the comb.[6]

---

6. Escrivá, *Friends of God*, no. 18.

To the active, zealous apostle this might seem counterintuitive. But our recurring sports motif comes again to the rescue here. The training of the body is essential for competition. Only comedies portray the unskilled taking on the more trained, the more athletic competitor. Grossly outmatching another is a joke; underestimating an opponent and overestimating oneself is a recipe for laughter in disaster, if we keep to the comedic angle.

David's defeat of Goliath is not the classic exception to the rule; it's not the story of a kid who got lucky, but of one who faced his adversary with the Lord's wisdom and strength, and God's weakness is more powerful than human strength. David was outmatched only in build and fierceness, but not in courage and skill, nor especially in faith.

The soul, not unlike the body, requires training. But the training is not the mere repetition of the acts of "solid piety" mentioned by St. Josemaría above. It is allowing them to penetrate the soul so that one begins to take on the likeness of Christ: to have his mind, his gaze, his words, his touch. Our own clumsy selves accomplish nothing if not elevated by the grace of Christ's self. We might remain rough and awkward in several ways, but Christ can even take these qualities and make them endearing to others.

Anyone can distribute food, medicine, or clothing, and visit the sick or imprisoned as the gospel demands we

do. But the gospel never stops at the outward act. Jesus
continually drills inward so that we never use external
works to cloak an inward emptiness, most especially not
to disguise hypocrisy. Good, selfless works from a pure
heart are what he wants because that is how he gives to us:
"You received without pay, give without pay" (Mt 10:8).

The trouble with active works, and activity in
general, is not that they eventually tire us out and
leave us either wanting a break or greater variety in
our activity. The problem is more than enduring the
boredom that accompanies repetition: it is misconstruing
work to be its own end and investing ourselves in it in
such a way that our minds, hearts, souls, and strength
alienate themselves from the Lord. Perhaps Judas had
this problem, among others. But one need not be an
out-and-out traitor to fall into what popes and spiritual
authors condemn as *activism*.[7]

Everyone acknowledges on paper that activism, that
is, activity unsupported by prayer, is a grave mistake and
contrary to the order of grace. Relatively few can stop
themselves in the midst of their activity to prove it. And

---

7. See, for example, Benedict XVI, Encyclical on Christian Love *Deus Caritas Est*
(December 25, 2005), nos. 36–38, Vatican website, www.vatican.va; Joseph Ratzinger
and Vittorio Messori, *The Ratzinger Report* (San Francisco: Ignatius, 1985), 103. These
and other warning voices on the dangers of activism may be found helpfully culled in
Dr. Peter Kwasniewski's *Ministers of Christ: Recovering the Roles of Clergy and Laity in
an Age of Confusion* (Manchester, N.H.: Crisis, 2021), especially in the chapter entitled
"Confronting the Heresy of Activism with the Primacy of Prayer."

that proof would be giving our minds, hearts, souls, and strength back to God in an exclusive way in prayer. It means spending time doing nothing else than being with God—keeping feet and hands still and, what is perhaps more difficult, keeping mind and heart at rest.

> [O]ur life of prayer should also be based on some moments that are dedicated exclusively to our conversation with God, moments of silent dialogue, before the tabernacle if possible, in order to thank our Lord for having waited for us—so often alone—for twenty centuries. This heart-to-heart dialogue with God is mental prayer, in which the whole soul takes part; intelligence, imagination, memory and will are all involved. It is a meditation that helps to give supernatural value to our poor human life, with all its normal, everyday occurrences.

> Thanks to these moments of meditation and to our vocal prayer and aspirations, we will be able to turn our whole day into a continuous praise of God, in a natural way and without any outward display. Just as people in love are always thinking about each other, we will be aware of God's presence. And all our actions, down to the most insignificant, will be filled with spiritual effectiveness.

> This is why, as a Christian sets out on his way of uninterrupted dealing with our Lord, his interior life grows and becomes strong and secure. And he

is led to engage in the demanding yet attractive struggle to fulfil completely the will of God. I might add that this is not a path for a privileged few; it is a way open to everyone.[8]

What is at stake is the full development of our human and divine potential. Subtract the dedication to prayer, beautifully described by our coach, and you're left with an anemic existence, unworthy of the name Christian. Just doing our duty each day is good, but also not sufficiently deep to be anything close to evangelical. What makes our ordinary workaday lives truly extraordinary is suffusing them with the spirit of Christ—his spirit in us, his words, thoughts, and actions reflected in ours. When the Lord teaches, for example, about how "one will be taken and the other left" at his coming in judgment, he is speaking of two people doing exactly the same thing outwardly (grinding at the mill or sleeping in a bed), and yet something *interior* clearly differentiates them (Mt 24:36–44; Lk 17:22–37). We can draw no other conclusion than that one was interiorly with God and the other more or less distant from him.

Thus, for the apostle, "Without interior life, and without formation, there is no true apostolate and no work that is fruitful. Whatever work is done will be fragile, fictitious even."[9]

---

8. Josemaría Escrivá, *Christ Is Passing By* (New York: Scepter, 2002), no. 119.
9. Josemaría Escrivá, *The Forge* (New York: Scepter, 2002), no. 892.

Two

What Work Is All About

There is no other way . . . either we learn to find our Lord in ordinary, everyday life, or we shall never find him.[10]

Caricatures in the spiritual life are easy to draw but not particularly helpful. They, like a street artist's caricatured portrait, purposely distort features to make them appear comical or ridiculous. Perceived exaggerations in the spiritual life lead one to say about another: "All he ever does is pray," or "All she ever does is work." A monster is thus created: the prayer or work monster—unstoppable, implacable, bent on doing one thing only.

---

10. Josemaría Escrivá, *Passionately Loving the World: A Homily Given on October 8, 1967* (New York: Scepter, 2002), p. 6.

On either side of prayer or work you have potential exaggerations. Those prone to one side or the other are liable to straw man their counterpart and tear them down, perhaps using (selectively) Scripture or the words of saints to support themselves. In either case, a partial truth is asserted above the fuller truth. It is always easier to know a small portion of truth really well than to take the time to interest oneself in other, equally valid points of view.

Yes, we all know the Lord's words about vine and branches, and that without him we can do nothing. Thus, prayerful and heartfelt union is demanded of the disciple. But we know equally well the Lord's teaching about works on display shining before men (and yet remaining a matter of practical indifference to the doer, whose left hand is kept in the dark over his right hand's doings). Thus is activity blessed and commanded of the disciple.

It is worth noting, as much for lay people as for any consecrated religious reading this book, that religious institutes given to both "contemplation and action" find the tension between the two a source of personal struggle and of community policy debates. For that matter, it might come as a surprise to know that purely contemplative monasteries struggle in comparable ways to balance work with periods of prayer. It makes one stop and ask whether an impossible balancing act is in question, and whether it might not be better just to give in to the caricature and devote oneself entirely to one thing. At least one would be spared having to think and discern each day how to spend one's time. But falling into this trap also "spares" us from seeking God's will, and to excuse ourselves from this discernment is nothing short of death to the soul.

The distortion souls of prayer might create is the tendency to so emphasize times of prayer that they predispose themselves to laziness or immobility. St. Josemaría accounts for this disorder in no. 734 of *The Forge*:

> People have often drawn attention to the danger of deeds performed without any interior life to inspire them; but we should also stress the danger of an interior life—if such a thing is possible— without deeds.

Doing nothing and resenting the call to be busy about the house like Martha because one feels too disconcerted in managing things, dealing with people, and being in complicated situations—this points to a spiritual immaturity that most people pass through as they figure out how prayer and work practically interface. Not knowing how they dovetail, or how to make them blend together, creates tension and frustration, sometimes leading to an abandonment of one or the other.

Of course, in the iconic example of Martha and Mary, the Lord condemns neither sister, but instead accentuates a spirit that needs to be present in both: Mary's wise and focused spirit needs to operate in Martha as well. Martha should keep working, but with her heart preoccupied, not with anxieties, but with pleasing the Lord.

The inability to be physically busy, working amid distraction and sometimes chaos, while remaining recollected—this state of affairs cannot endure if one is to grow spiritually, if one is to maintain both balance and sanity.

> No, my children! We cannot lead a double life. We cannot have a split personality, if we want to be Christians. There is only one life, made of flesh and spirit. And it is that life which has to become, in both body and soul, holy and filled with God: we discover the invisible God in the most visible and material things.
>
> There is no other way, my daughters and sons: either we learn to find our Lord in ordinary, everyday life, or we shall never find him.[11]

Our finding of the Lord hinges on our ability to do all things in him, with him, and through him. "All things" means both prayer and works done together, even if prayer must precede and accompany all that we do in the Lord's name. And even if our prayer is the objectively better thing to do, it cannot restrict itself to set times, but

---

11. Escrivá, *Passionately Loving the World*, p. 6.

must thoroughly saturate our entire day. Otherwise, how can we pray always, as the Scriptures enjoin us to?

On this score, St. Teresa of Ávila, in her typically direct manner, sets straight her fellow cloistered Carmelites:

> The true lover loves everywhere and is always thinking of the Beloved! It would be a thing hard to bear if we were able to pray only when off in some corner. I do realize that prayer in the midst of occupations cannot last many hours; but, O my Lord, what power over You a sigh of sorrow has that comes from the depths of our hearts on seeing that it isn't enough that we are in this exile but that we are not even given the chance to be alone enjoying You.[12]

Loving everywhere and always thinking of the Beloved gets at the heart of action permeated by contemplation. Those who downplay the importance of contemplation in the apostolic life might very well caricature it as daydreaming, idle thinking, time wasting, and so forth. But to contemplate rightly, one must be prepared for battle—not simply the struggle to concentrate, but to focus the mind and heart on God so as to listen to and follow him. It is getting our love right, or ordering our

---

12. St. Teresa of Ávila, *The Book of Her Foundations*, in *The Collected Works of St. Teresa of Ávila*, vol. 3, trans. Kieran Kavanaugh and Otilio Rodriguez, rev. ed. (Washington, D.C.: ICS, 1987), p. 123.

love by discerning where our hearts tend, where thoughts drift to, and rectifying them accordingly.

Nothing proves where our hearts are, what we really want, where our treasure lies, like activity does.

God puts man into a world furnished with a hierarchical order of beautiful creatures, all of which were intended to speak ceaselessly to man about the perfections of God, all of which should lead man's heart to desire God. After the original sin, however, man became blinded to the inherently divine orientation of creation, so that the world now has the awful power to *keep us far from God*.

St Josemaría would preach frequently and vigorously not only that this unnatural separation must end, but that the Incarnation itself has already put a stop to it. Christians need to receive this fact with open arms and let it transform their lives, as it so profoundly changed the lives of the first generations of disciples. His famous homily *Passionately Loving the World*, already quoted above, is perhaps where these themes are distilled most forcefully:

> Our age needs to give back to matter and to the apparently trivial events and of life their noble, original meaning. It needs to place them at the service of the kingdom of God; it needs to spiritualize them, turning them into a means and

an occasion for a continuous meeting with Jesus
Christ.[13]

To think otherwise makes our spiritual lives, and
our Christian faith in general, things ill-suited to this
world. Fallen people like ourselves are often tempted to
compartmentalize areas of life that we find difficult to put
together, like prayer and work, or love of God and love
of neighbor.

Finding the divine in the human calls for an active
faith, a lively desire to see what God wants us to see. What
human eyes would never notice without grace to illumine
them is precisely what we must keep in focus.

This calls for an essentially contemplative vision of
life, "in the middle of the street," as St Josemaría often
repeated. Just as the people of Jesus' time had to look
beyond (not disregard) his human appearance in order
to see God, so must we arrive at a clarity that leads us
to the treasure buried in an otherwise nondescript field.
The sameness that characterizes most of our relationships
and activities is the unspectacular setting in which God
chooses to reveal himself.

Work, then, is what? A duty? Yes. It is a burden laid
upon all the children of Adam—originally a sweet burden
and privilege before original sin made it onerous and often

---

13. Escrivá, *Passionately Loving the World*, p. 6.

fruitless. But as a specifically Christian duty, it is an act of conformity to the New Adam, and therefore an act of worship of the incarnate Word. Once God becomes man in Christ, all that we do in imitation of him, all that we do to bring our bent-up and broken humanity to be perfect like his, becomes acts of holy love, devotion, and

> a living sacrifice, holy and acceptable to God, which is your spiritual worship. Do not be conformed to this world but be transformed by the renewal of your mind, that you may prove what is the will of God, what is good and acceptable and perfect. (Rom 12:1–2)

Three

Rest, Recreation, & Renewal: Luxury or Duty?

Times of rest or recreation . . . are as important
in our daily lives as is work itself.[14]

What I identified as a problem in the foregoing chapters—the precedence of work or apostolate over prayer—sets us up for further problems. Accordingly, a brief chapter on the sometimes ambiguous character of those moments between work and prayer that we give to rest and recreation is in order. "Ambiguous" for a couple of reasons.

First, because some feel guilty or useless whenever they're not doing something. Either they consider it an imperfection to play or rest, or a waste of time not to

---

14. Escrivá, *Friends of God*, no. 10.

have material results to show for time spent doing . . . nothing. It was likely to these that St. Josemaría directed his comment:

> Certainly it is necessary to rest, because we have to tackle our work each day with renewed vigor. But, as I wrote many years ago, "to rest is not to do nothing. It is to turn our attention to other activities that require less effort."[15]

Or to someone completely depleted and needing to be told it's okay to cease and desist for a time:

> Physical collapse. You are worn out. Rest. Stop that exterior activity. Consult a doctor. Obey, and don't worry.
>
> You will soon return to your normal life and, if you are faithful, to new intensity in your apostolate.[16]

Nothing inhuman here, but rather a clear recognition of the limits of the human machine to work or do anything without sufficient rest. Here is your reminder, if you need it. If you cite those instances when St. Josemaría praises "work without rest,"[17] let's be clear that he does not mean "never rest," but that when we work, we should be tireless in our efforts. In other words, to do everything

---

15. Escrivá, *Friends of God*, no. 62.

16. Escrivá, *The Way*, no. 706.

17. For example, see Escrivá, *The Way*, no. 373; Escrivá, *The Forge*, no. 65.

with its proper intensity. It is the same in physical training or working out: you push through your reps, you sprint with all your might, because if you rest while doing either, you never make progress. It's only after you've spent your energy that rest is in order. Consider: "By neglecting small details you could work on and on without rest and yet live the life of a perfect idler."[18] Lacking the intensity and diligence proper to our work turns work into a hobby or pastime instead of a divine work.

The second ambiguity regards the value of what we call recreation. Not all diversions are created equal: if it becomes self-indulgence or dissipation, no renewal of spirit is possible. "Renewal is not relaxation"[19] is St. Josemaría's way of saying that simply to slacken our efforts, although providing rest for the body, does nothing to refresh the soul. Relaxation, in other words, does not automatically replenish the soul with inspiration and zeal. Hence, for the apostle, how we spend our downtime matters as much as how we act when we're "on."

Clearly, every exertion creates a need for rest and repair, even for the zealous apostle. The Lord sanctions such rest when he calls his men away for a little while to recuperate after their work. Significantly, his insistence comes on the heels of the apostles' enthusiastic report

18. Escrivá, *Furrow*, no. 494.
19. Escrivá, *Furrow*, no. 176.

regarding "all that they had done and taught" (Mk 6:30). The Lord's response isn't, "Great work! Now get back out there and keep going!" He responds as much to their need for humility as to their need to renew themselves in solitude. In other words, although joy and gratitude are called for when we have accomplished what God has given us to do, the apostle must take great care not to rest in his accomplishments.

They had been handling some tremendous power: casting out "many demons" and healing "many that were sick" (Mk 6:13). Or, as the seventy disciples exclaim, "Lord, even the demons are subject to us in your name!" (Lk 10:17). To press pause in the midst of all this success seems counterintuitive. Why not keep going, keep exorcising and healing? Because inevitably a fallen man begins to believe that he commands the power that flows through him. Better not do anything than do a lot of good things with God on the end of your leash.

For this reason, St. Josemaría puts "rest or recreation" on equal footing with work itself. That's saying a lot. It is also saying something that St. Thomas Aquinas saw fit to address in the *Summa*:

> Just as man needs bodily rest for the body's refreshment, because he cannot always be at work, since his power is finite and equal to a certain fixed amount of labor, so too is it with his soul, whose

power is also finite and equal to a fixed amount of work. Consequently when he goes beyond his measure in a certain work, he is oppressed and becomes weary, and all the more since when the soul works, the body is at work likewise.[20]

St. Thomas also cites the classic example of the archer, an apocryphal story of St. John the Apostle, recorded in the *Conferences* of St. John Cassian:

When some people were scandalized on finding [St. John] playing together with his disciples, he is said to have told one of them who carried a bow to shoot an arrow. And when the latter had done this several times, he asked him whether he could do it indefinitely, and the man answered that if he continued doing it, the bow would break. Whence the Blessed John drew the inference that in like manner man's mind would break if its tension were never relaxed.[21]

Tension inevitably strains both mind and body as one concentrates on the details of work, striving to do a good job. But releasing that tension is indispensable. People who never give themselves this permission do

20. Thomas Aquinas, *Summa Theologica* 2-2.168.2, resp, in *The Summa Theologiae of St. Thomas Aquinas*, trans. Fathers of the English Dominican Province, 2nd and rev. ed. (1920; online ed. Kevin Knight, 2017), https://www.newadvent.org/summa/3168.htm#article2.

21. Aquinas, *Summa Theologica* 2-1.168.2, resp, in *The Summa Theologiae of St. Thomas Aquinas*. See St. John Cassian, *Conference 24*, par. 21: Conference of Abbot Abraham on Mortification.

eventually break. And sometimes this brings discredit upon themselves and the work they've been busy about.

But will just any type of relaxation do? St. Josemaría warns against what spiritual authors call *dissipation*, the antithesis of recreation:

> Dissipation—You slake your senses and faculties in whatever pool you meet on the way. And you can feel the results: unsettled purpose, scattered attention, deadened will, and quickened concupiscence.
>
> Subject yourself once again to a serious plan that will make you lead a Christian life: or you'll never do anything worthwhile.[22]

This tells me that recreation needs to be more than idleness. It must be directed by intentionality. What am I trying to get out of a period of non-work? Trouble comes when the sought-out recreation is really more distracting or dissipating than rejuvenating. Or when Christian apostles begin to "live for the weekend," rather than living for Christ and receiving days of rest as his gift.

Here we cannot pass over the almost universal practice of resorting to scrolling on the cell phone, watching Internet videos, seeking to gratify curiosity by looking up largely irrelevant things; these are those stagnant "pools"

---

22. Escrivá, *The Way*, no. 375.

we meet along the way. What begins as a pastime ends as a mindless habit, crowding any free moment with images and noise. I'm not aware of anyone who feels less tense and more aware of God's presence afterwards, which is what apostles need to be concerned about.

> You play around with temptations, you put yourself in danger, you fool around with your sight and with your imagination, you chat about . . . stupidities. And then you are anxious that doubts, scruples, confusion, sadness, and discouragement might assail you.
>
> You must admit that you are not very consistent.[23]

I'm not condemning Internet use wholesale for all of the good things that one may find on it, even some types of healthy diversion. But what I cannot see as healthy, much less refreshing for the soul, is the mindless dependence on changing images, videos, and information of which the Internet is made. Having this as your go-to for recreation is to sabotage the very purpose of seeking it in the first place.

It's important to bring this out into the open, since unlike alcohol or drug abuse (and certainly unlike consumption of pornography), Internet use is largely

---

23. Escrivá, *Furrow*, no. 132.

morally neutral, since content depends mostly on the user. Few would really question the morality of spending several aimless hours online. We can sometimes excuse ourselves from discipline and mortification in media or information consumption. But the addictive quality of this remains a danger for anyone intent on building an interior life. In all fairness, I might add that people can do the same type of thing, the same type of idle browsing, in library stacks. Digital meandering is just quicker.

If this is the main diversion offered to us by the modern world, we need to have healthier alternatives that counter the isolating nature of disordered Internet use. For recreation to live up to its name, we should seek other people with whom we can recreate (i.e., not just wish to be left alone so that we can gratify curiosity online). We get our emotional needs met in community, not in isolation. And recreation is nothing if not a way of developing and enjoying emotions that we put on hold during work.

But on a deeper level, we need to seek renewal in God. We have dwelt on this point already, but perhaps as a practical application we need to schedule days or hours of prayer, of retreat. An annual retreat, a monthly evening of recollection, a daily holy hour before the Blessed Sacrament—taken together, these renew the soul of the apostle. When we go to the source of life, we are rejuvenated, made youthful again in spirit.

When we return to work, we find a new spirit emerging in us. We bring to work a broader sense of God's presence and providence in the events of the day. We find the day's happenings feeding our prayer life, in fact leading us into prayer in the midst of our activity. Christ begins to appear in places we never thought to expect him.

What seems like a waste of time to some, the taking of time away for rest and renewal, is really a way of taking stock of what we do during business hours. Do we just assume that it's all pleasing to God because our "stats" are impressive? Is it all about numbers?

> You can climb to the top of your profession, you can gain the highest acclaim as a reward for your freely chosen endeavors in temporal affairs; but if you abandon the supernatural outlook that should inspire all our human activities, you will have gone sadly astray.[24]

What we gain in those periods of recreation and of spiritual renewal is a reawakening of love for the apostolate. If apostolate is the specific work a Christian carries out in the world to make Christ known and loved, then we ourselves must first be filled with that love. Its absence makes whatever work we do something very

---

24. Escrivá, *Friends of God*, no. 10.

different from apostolate. It might be anything from drudgery to elated success at the "top of your profession," but whatever it is, if love is missing, it is not Christian.

> All that exterior activity is a waste of time, if you lack Love. It's like sewing with a needle and no thread.
>
> What a pity if in the end you had carried out "your" apostolate and not "his" apostolate![25]

Resting reminds the gospel laborer that he is neither irreplaceable nor the main attraction. It is St. Josemaría's saying all over again: "I have to pass unnoticed and disappear, so that Jesus alone may be in the limelight."[26] And nothing makes us more unnoticed than withdrawing for a while from the sight of men to do something like our Lord himself did: pray alone in deserted places or go off alone with his apostles simply to enjoy time with them.

---

25. Escrivá, *The Way*, no. 967.
26. Salvador Bernal, *Msgr. Josemaría Escrivá de Balaguer: A Profile of the Founder of Opus Dei* (London and New York: Scepter, 1977), p. 10.

Four

Not for Your Coffee Mug: The Unquotable St. Josemaría

Don't forget that you are just a trash can.[27]

Whenever I use this point from *The Way* in retreat conferences, people visibly balk at it. I concede, often to giggles, that it may not be the kind of inspirational quote you would want on your coffee mug. But the perplexity remains. How can a saint say something like this? Yet this saint, and others too numerous to list, say such things. For that matter, as we shall see, so do our Lord and the New Testament authors.

---

27. Escrivá, *The Way*, no. 592.

I don't blame people for finding it repugnant. Taken at face value, it sounds like an insult, a put-down, or a dismissal of one's dignity. In full, the quote reads:

> Don't forget that you are just a trash can. So if by any chance the divine gardener should lay his hands on you, and scrub and clean you, and fill you with magnificent flowers, neither the scent nor the colors that beautify your ugliness should make you proud.
>
> Humble yourself: don't you know that you are a trash can?[28]

Of course, taking everything at face value is not what disciples do, because they are contemplatives at heart: looking, pondering, considering in the light of faith. If the Lord complains of people without eyes to see and ears to hear, it is not against the blind and deaf he inveighs, but against those who, thinking they see and hear quite well, lack understanding. The secrets of the kingdom are revealed precisely to the childlike, that is, to those who gaze in wonder at the *magnalia Dei*.[29]

---

28. Escrivá, *The Way*, no. 592. The Spanish is no less severe: "No olvides que eres . . . el depósito de la basura—Por eso, si acaso el Jardinero divino echa mano de ti, y te friega y te limpia . . . y te llena de magníficas flores, . . . ni el aroma ni el color, que embellecen tu fealdad, han de ponerte orgulloso—Humíllate: ¿no sabes que eres el cacharro de los desperdicios?

29. The "great things" or "wonders of God," from Sirach 18:6, also cited by St. Josemaría in the last paragraphs of *Passionately Loving the World*. In Vulgate: 18:5.

After all, Jesus' own saying about "unworthy" or "useless" servants (Lk 17:7–10) might come across to the unreflective hearer as both ungrateful and discourteous. But prayer and reflection may yield a truer reading, something akin to "[D]o not let your left hand know what your right hand is doing" (Mt 6:3), and so fill out the meaning. Far from implying "just do what you're told and get lost," the Lord's directive to his servants has everything to do with loving and giving as God loves and gives: without drawing attention to oneself, and even without distinction for good and evil people (see Mt 5:43–48).

Taking the case even further, let's not forget what St. Paul says about Christ in his abasement as man: "[God] made him to be sin who knew no sin" (2 Cor 5:21). And of course, Isaiah's prophecy graphically illustrates what it means "to be sin":

> [H]e had no form or comeliness that we should look at him,
>   and no beauty that we should desire him.
> He was despised and rejected by men;
>   a man of sorrows, and acquainted with grief;
> and as one from whom men hide their faces
>   he was despised, and we esteemed him not.
> Surely he has borne our griefs
>   and carried our sorrows;
> yet we esteemed him stricken,
>   smitten by God, and afflicted.

But he was wounded for our transgressions,
    he was bruised for our iniquities;
upon him was the chastisement that made us whole,
    and with his stripes we are healed. (Is 53:2–5)

Jesus smeared himself with our ugliness, made himself the "receptacle" of human garbage, which is our "transgressions" and "iniquities." And the language of "despised and rejected" is precisely how we regard garbage itself: something rejected, unwanted, distasteful to look at. Yet Isaiah applies this to the Person of Jesus Christ.

Any feathers ruffled over St. Josemaría's point should now gently fall back into place. We cannot place ourselves lower than the Son of God did for us in becoming man, emptying himself, and taking the form of a slave (see Phil 2:5–7). "Think about it slowly," St. Josemaría guides us, "He, being God, humiliated himself; man, puffed up with self-love, tries to build himself up at any cost, without recognizing that he is but a creature of clay, and poor clay at that."[30]

Perhaps looking at this from the angle of love will also fill in any gaps left over. "When you are in love," writes Fr. Bede Jarrett, "you realize how humbling love is."

---

30. Escrivá, *Friends of God*, no. 112.

You realize when you are in love what a very little you have to bring to the one you love. Friendship, while it exalts you, makes you realize the poverty of your own heart, the emptiness of your own soul, you wish you had much more to bring, much more of yourself, a finer character, a worthier gift. This humility will be found in divine love too. Once you awake to the knowledge of what God is you realize how very little you have to offer Him. You want to give Him at least all of the little that is yours.[31]

Now back to that empty trash can. Rather than passing over the apparent awkwardness of the saint's saying, let's engage it and see what it can teach us. It may go contrary to all of the cultural and personal work we've done to affirm children, build the self-esteem of teenagers, and counsel doubtful adults about their purpose in life, but it flows quite naturally and unembarrassedly from the pen of a saint. Is it his problem or ours?

Allowing for the fact that many, if not most of the points of *The Way* were extracted from letters and conversations of spiritual direction, we should avoid reading it as though it had no original context. In the case of no. 592, moreover, the origin of it is striking: it comes from Escrivá's personal prayer, a self-directed comment

---

31. Bede Jarrett, OP, *No Abiding City* (London: Burns, Oates, & Washbourne, 1938), pp. 45–46.

from his own journal.[32] His first application, in other words, is to himself.

In speaking to himself, he gives no quarter to pride, the particular pride a priest is susceptible to. We do many great things in the Lord's name, and as people praise us for inspiring and changing their lives, the instinct of a fallen man is to attribute the good to himself. St. Paul is very clear on the absurdity of this. The good results not from my charismatic personality, eloquence, quick wittedness, charm, or whatever. "Only God . . . gives the growth" (1 Cor 3:7).

We should only take gospel success or fecundity as far as an old priest once advised me after a moment of success: "All the glory goes to God. But it's nice to know we cooperated." Enough said. Thank God he shares his work with us and move on.

If attributing to ourselves the good we do is the fallen man's knee-jerk response, then it needs to be replaced by a higher instinct, a truer reflex motion. Joy is that spontaneous response. I mean that if the garbage can imagery provokes sadness, it is because we don't perceive the joy in our poverty.

---

32. See Josemaría Escrivá, *The Way: Critical-Historical Edition*, ed. Pedro Rodríguez (New York: Scepter, 2010), p. 761.

Put not the slightest trust in those who present the virtue of humility as something degrading, or as a virtue condemning us to a permanent state of dejection. To know we are made of clay, riveted together again, is a continual source of joy. It means acknowledging our littleness in the eyes of God: a little child, a son. Can there be any joy to compare with that of the person who, knowing himself to be poor and weak, knows also that he is a son of God? Why do we men become dejected? It is because life on earth does not go the way we had hoped, or because obstacles arise which prevent us from satisfying our personal ambitions.[33]

If, instead, we cling to vain ideas of self-worth and try to amass accomplishments as so many testimonials to our dignity, greatness, or both, then dejection and bitterness are ever close at hand. All it takes is for one plan to fall through, or some lack of appreciation or approval, and we are demoralized. Right away we are vexed: "What's the point?," we ask. It's an open question, but one whose answer isn't a doubling down on our efforts and more repetition until we succeed. That would only feed the bad motive. And people with bad motives sometimes succeed famously, without in the least improving themselves before God.

---

33. Escrivá, *Friends of God*, no. 108.

The answer is prayerful reflection and honest examination of oneself. *Why did I fail? Is there something about a success that might be harmful?* Sometimes, even at the cost of some attainment, the Lord lets our efforts fail because our success would be our downfall.

The point, as was said earlier, is that the apostolate is "his" and not "mine." So that both success and failure come as the Lord wills. Joy in success and sadness in failure are human and natural. Dejection, on the other hand, means that too much self-esteem was riding on some project, and when it failed, I fell along with it like a tragic hero. The same is true of success, when we are overly elated by some triumph. Rejoice, yes, but rejoice in the Lord, give thanks to him, bless his name. Only in heaven will our victory be secure, everlasting, and totally void of self-regard.

If I've been operating on other principles or going after goals other than Christian ones, it's just a matter of time before my house collapses. Or, what is just as likely, I will collapse even if my work is wildly successful. Why? Because anything less than God will never, can never, satisfy us. I wonder how many times throughout our lives we need to hear that lesson again? I wonder how many times a coach needs to shout it to us from the sidelines?

Everything depends on the foundation I stand on. If it is some form of self, or some rickety structure I've built up, it cannot bear the weight of the Christian apostolate. We're dealing with a power that is not of this world, with ends that go far beyond the horizon. And do I really think I can just approach discipleship and apostolate like any other business venture? Do I really think I can measure success and failure in the same ways corporations do?

We begin the life of discipleship poor, and our goal is to remain poor, even to grow in poverty. With eyes taken off of self, with no pretensions to excellence, with a simple joy that God notices me at all and delights to use me in some small corner of his kingdom . . . yes, I will be a garbage can in the Lord's kingdom any day. Put me on some street in his city, preferably a backstreet, and I will serve there, awaiting his cleansing and beautifying of my very ordinary self.

Five

Clay Made Divine: Material for Sanctity

Ever since I began to preach, I have warned people against a certain mistaken sense of holiness. Don't be afraid to know your real self. That's right, you are made of clay. Don't be worried. For you and I are sons of God—and that is the right way of being made divine.[34]

An objection is raised from the preceding chapter: But what if I go on feeling like a garbage can, minus the scrubbing and the flowers? Or what if I just feel like garbage? If you do, it is likely because of deficient knowledge of self and

---

34. Escrivá, *Christ is Passing By*, no. 160.

of God. To know you are a sinner takes no special insight, but to know *that* God loves sinners, *how* he loves them, and *why* he loves them, does. To have some understanding of why the shepherd leaves the ninety-nine sheep in search of you, and rejoices to find you, this takes something beyond ordinary insight.

> "Father, how can you listen to such filth?" you asked me, after a contrite confession.
>
> I said nothing, and thought that if your humility makes you feel like that—filth: a heap of filth!—we may yet turn all your weakness into something really great.[35]

Wretchedness must coexist with sanctification in the Christian life. That is, the saint never ceases to be a sinner, never ceases to have defects. They become fewer, to be sure, and certainly less grave; and yet another paradox emerges: the closer we get to God, the more misery we see in ourselves. His holiness lights up all of our dark corners, leaving nothing unexposed.

> You are dust—fallen and dirty. Even though the breath of the holy Spirit should lift you above all the things of the earth and make you shine like gold, as your misery reflects in those heights the

---

sovereign rays of the Sun of Justice, do not forget the lowliness of your state.[36]

We don't forget our misery but we also don't let it sink us into despair. Knowing ourselves, as St. Josemaría frequently insists, we're none too impressed. We might even get *de*pressed with each increase in self-knowledge. Escrivá accounts for this with a simple solution: "If you feel depressed when you experience, perhaps in a very vivid way, your own pettiness, then is the time to abandon yourself completely and obediently into God's hands."[37] There's more to this than meets the eye. Abandoning oneself means to give or entrust oneself to another without restraint, putting oneself into the other's hands with complete vulnerability and trust. Why do this with God?

Because, left to ourselves, we have no better solution to the "garbage" problem except doing what fallen people do best: "stupidly" priding ourselves on our gifts, trying to build ourselves up at any cost, failing to come to terms with our status as clay vessels.[38] Hubert van Zeller, St. Josemaría's contemporary, reflects on this in connection with Ash Wednesday, the ultimate liturgical reminder of

---

36. Escrivá, *The Way*, no. 599.
37. Escrivá, *Christ Is Passing By*, no. 160.
38. See Escrivá, *Friends of God*, no. 112.

our need to be real, as real as dirt, dust, ash, clay, whatever we call the element we all revert to in the end.

> "Remember, man, that thou art dust, and unto dust thou shalt return." There are implications to be found in this. If man had been fashioned from something that could evaporate, there would be nothing for him to return to. But a man, even while he is living in the flesh, can return to his constituent element: he does this the moment he is ready to be what God has made him. Dust may not be romantic, but there could be nothing more real.[39]

Both of these giants of the spiritual life insist we get real or get comfortable being who we really are—not depressed, but humbly joyful in being what God has made us to be. This self, whether male or female, which we assert, dramatize, panic over, or protect, this self needs such a solemn and earthy reminder as black ash rubbed into the forehead because it tends to live too much in unreality, or in a self-made reality. At our worst and most insecure, we attempt to recreate ourselves apart from God's purpose for us. Do we not feel strangely relieved when someone looks us in the eye and says, "Just be yourself"? This is what our good coach keeps calling us back to.

---

39. Hubert van Zeller, *The Choice of God* (London: Burns & Oates, 1956), p. 41.

But to know what it means "to be yourself" means knowing not only that you are a weak sinner, but also what Christ's Death and Resurrection do to your sins and weaknesses. Someone needs to tell us, to shout it at close range until we get it, that real change is possible, real repentance, real conversion and growth.

Our coach asks on his behalf and ours for these practical gifts:

> Lord, from now on let me become someone else: no longer "me," but that "other person" you would like me to be.
>
> Let me not deny you anything you ask of me. Let me know how to pray. Let me know how to suffer. Let me not worry about anything except your glory. Let me feel your presence all the time.
>
> May I love the Father. May I hunger for you, my Jesus, in a permanent Communion. May the Holy Spirit set me on fire.[40]

It is not enough to know ourselves. That's half of the equation, and not the most appealing half. Necessary, but incomplete. We need to know the Lord. St. Augustine gets the equation right: "Let me know myself, let me know You."[41] St. Bernard of Clairvaux asserts love as the

---

40. Escrivá, *The Forge*, no. 122.

41. Augustine of Hippo, *Soliloquies*, 2.1, in *Nicene and Post-Nicene Fathers*, First Series, vol. 7, ed. Philip Schaff, trans. C. C. Starbuck (Buffalo, N.Y.: Christian Literature Publishing, 1888; online ed. Kevin Knight), https://www.newadvent.org/fathers/170302.htm.

catalyst for this essential knowledge, saying with great depth that only when we love God with our whole minds, hearts, and strength do we experience our true selves as being unlovable, except insofar as we belong to God. As we feel drawn to him, so do we simultaneously see the inadequacies of self, and how radically our self-love must depend on his for us.[42]

So, there is an undeniable sense in which we see ourselves as less than nothing the closer we are to God. The garbage can imagery may be brusque and off-putting, but only truly debilitating if it is divorced from Love, from the God who is Love. His love makes us who we truly are, who we are meant to be. If we see ourselves as basically fine and complete without God, we leave very little room for growth. Actually, we see a complete distortion: we are not even close to our true selves, our best selves, until we first completely humble ourselves before the Lord. Only those prostrate on the earth can be lifted up, only they can be exalted, only the least and last can be first.

Here is the tricky paradox: To become "divine," as St. Josemaría indicates above, we must first acknowledge that we are absolutely nothing without God, even "worth nothing," as he often says about himself. But at the same time, this "nothing" is the material out of which the Lord

---

42. See Bernard of Clairvaux, *Sermons on the Song of Songs*, vol. 3 (Kalamazoo, Mich.: Cistercian Publications, 1979), pp. 35–36.

makes sons of God, heirs to eternal glory, coheirs with Christ. Hence, our holy coach says, "Don't be worried," because this is "the right way of being made divine."[43]

Sin locks us into a toxic state of mind, a mind depressed at its own nothingness, weakness, and frailty, by blinding us to a Love that loves us in our place of dejection. If we don't believe that God can love something so faulty as ourselves, we have failed to know the depth of his mercy: "He raises up the poor from the dust; he lifts the needy from the ash heap, to make them sit with princes and inherit a seat of honor" (1 Sm 2:8).

Sin numbs us to truth, beauty, and real love. Sin robs us of our sense of self-worth, our God-given dignity as his children. If we feel like garbage much of the time, we really have to question where that feeling comes from: Is it from God, the self, the world, or the devil? If the feeling discourages and renders us immobile in our journey, it is not of God. Rather, to feel like nothing and yet to rejoice in the goodness and mercy of God is a sign that our tricky paradox is beginning to make perfect sense to us.

---

43. Escrivá, *Christ is Passing By*, no. 160.

Six

Strong Language: The Tough Talk We Need

Make use of the "strong language apostolate."
The next time we meet I'll tell you—in a
whisper—a few useful words.[44]

A couple of generations ago, Hubert van Zeller, the great Benedictine spiritual writer whom we've quoted above, prefaced his book, *The Choice of God,* with a complaint: "The literature of spirituality is getting soft; spiritual people are accordingly getting soft."[45] For the record, that was in 1956.

---

44. Escrivá, *The Way*, no. 850.
45. Hubert van Zeller, *The Choice of God*, preface, p. vii.

This softness, he explains, issues from a selective reading of the Gospel: an emphasis on what consoles to the neglect of what challenges, and perhaps even frightens. Apologists have often observed that no one in the Bible speaks more about hell than Jesus, no one speaks more about the narrowness of the way that leads to life than he does—and indeed, the real impossibility of salvation unless one goes to the Father through him.

Every generation has its own particular spiritual needs, its own points of emphasis, and certainly its own distortions in the area of spirituality. Some generations, especially those affluent and complacent, need particularly stark reminders of God's judgment and of hell's eternal pains. Other generations, coming off of periods of great and traumatic suffering, need more of an incentive to trust in the Lord. Both of these emphases are found squarely in the Bible: God speaks to his people words of comfort or words of chastisement precisely when things have gotten, respectively, too hard or too soft.

Admittedly, I do not have a working knowledge of all that gets published under the category of "spirituality." Books on spirituality are legion and many of them lead down paths that do not end with Christ, and thus are dead in the water, whatever other helps they might offer. The emphasis on self and tapping into one's inner resources seems to be the focus and appeal of much of this. No need to involve a self-revealing God whose truths alone can save. It is much less threatening to advertise the self as God and promise a way to actualize your inner divinity. Where these books are not simply misguided, they are outright gnostic or cabalistic.

What do the children of this generation need? Nothing that will simply pass away once this generation does—a "throwaway" spirituality, in other words. With the gospel of Jesus, we are dealing with eternal truths that cannot expire nor ever be rendered irrelevant. We are not looking to bandage wounds, but to heal with a healing that goes deep beneath the surface. As unconsoling as this might sound, it needs saying that healing is seldom without pain—a pain St. John of the Cross frequently refers to as a "cautery." Healing burns, stings, wrings tears, and often leaves one feeling very weak. Yet if the healing comes from the Lord, it is never without hope of recovery. We need this pain, this discomfort, to receive healing fully.

We do not need "soft" spirituality that edits out the challenging parts of the gospel. Gagging the gospel so as not to put off the worldly or fainthearted does nothing but add to the sickness. Nor should the assurances and encouragement of the Scriptures be omitted in favor of instilling the fear of God in souls. We need a full gospel, exacting and comforting, and comforting precisely because in its demands we experience our frailty, and in its comfort we are encouraged to strive after higher things.

Reenter St. Josemaría.

I am deliberately accommodating the saint's words about the "strong language apostolate" to mean his uncompromisingly tough words to his spiritual sons and daughters. St. Josemaría is famous for not pulling punches. And as much as the punch might sting, sometimes we need to be stung to rise above ourselves. Our next chapter will illustrate how gentle, understanding, and encouraging our coach is. He never loses an opportunity to say how capable he himself is of committing the worst sins, drawing this important gospel conclusion from that fact. He understands everyone else's weaknesses based on his own. A lesson all of us need to take to heart: the deeper we are in self-knowledge, the deeper our compassion runs for the miseries of others.

But the tack St. Josemaría often takes is just as often one of challenge, since he also knows how powerful the grace of God is and what great things we are capable of. Like a good coach would.

It is well to mention that our coach can also take his own medicine. During his perilous escape from the so-called "Red Zone" of Republican Spain during the Civil War (1936–1939), he needed to be told by his refugee companions in no uncertain terms to continue the trek over the Pyrenees to Andorra, and then into France. The saint was so distressed over leaving some of his Opus Dei family behind in Madrid that, like a good father, he wanted to remain with them. Continually second-guessing himself, he was finally told by Juan Jiménez Vargas, "We're taking you to the other side, dead or alive."[46] That's the quotable portion. What Vargas said at a subsequent moment of Father's indecision, although not made explicit by him, was still an example of the "strong language apostolate":

> I panicked at the thought that he might decide to return. Without hesitation I grabbed his arm. I was not about to let him turn back, and I told him so in very crude, impolite language. I recall it with horror, but it was necessary, because I knew he had decided not to go on and I felt obliged to fight him on that.[47]

Sometimes the kind and gentle approach just won't do. To get someone's attention and to show them the seriousness of the situation, the verbal equivalent of smelling salts is sometimes in order.

The Lord himself was not averse to this. He fired back at those who delayed in following him that they

---

46. As quoted in Andrés Vázquez de Prada, *The Founder of Opus Dei*, vol. 2 (New York: Scepter, 2003), p. 145.
47. Vázquez de Prada, pp. 152–153.

were, respectively, "dead" or "unfit," while to another who pledged unconditionally to follow Jesus "wherever," he replied: but I have "nowhere" to call my own (Lk 9:57–62). These exchanges could have taken another direction, could have assumed a gentler tone, but the Lord willed to be tough—not to dissuade, but to make these men rise to the occasion.

In sports, coaches not infrequently "insult" their players to get them to perform better. Music teachers often employ the same technique to get their budding musicians to keep better pitch, time, and so forth. And perhaps even more famously, military drill instructors humiliate their recruits not only to motivate performance but also to toughen them. If you're not up for the challenge, you'll go away defeated and resentful, if not in tears.

A good put-down generates a healthy anger and goes a long way in pushing someone to go beyond themselves, to achieve what they didn't think possible. Admittedly, men tend to do this to each other more than women. I once heard a woman observe that "men bond by putting each other down," and there's no denying that. We knock each other around, call each other "dog" and "loser"—but always with a wink. We know what we're doing, even if it sounds mean. We're pushing each other to do better. Men soften if they go unchallenged, and so fail to attain not only a mature masculinity but also gospel greatness.

Is this what St. Josemaría is doing when he challenges the lukewarmness, laziness, and inconstancy of his reader with such firepower?

> Is it you who are creating that atmosphere of discontent among those around you?—Forgive me then for having to tell you that, apart from being bad, you are plain stupid.[48]

> You have not set yourself against God. Your falls are due to weakness. All right; but those weaknesses are so frequent—you aren't able to avoid them—that, if you don't want me to think you bad, I shall have to think you both bad and stupid.[49]

> With that self-satisfied air you are becoming an unbearable and repulsive character. You are making a fool of yourself, and, what is worse, you're diminishing the effect of your work as an apostle.

> Don't forget that even the mediocre can sin by being too scholarly.[50]

Bad, stupid, mediocre. Can you deal with that? The negativity of the motivation only works if you know something crucial: *that the one who challenges you loves you.* And he loves you not so that you will outperform

---

48. Escrivá, *Furrow*, no. 546.
49. Escrivá, *The Way*, no. 713.
50. Escrivá, *The Way*, no. 351.

an opponent and win a game, but to win a crown that never perishes.

It's one thing to belittle or shame another: these can be bullying tactics or spring from a need to assert oneself over others, to neutralize an opponent. But critical language in the spiritual life has nothing in common with this. It assumes a standard, a high standard, which one is not living up to, and *can live up to*.

In addition to knowing that your coach or teacher loves you and wills your betterment, you must also know something crucial about yourself: *You can do better. You are called to great holiness. Your vocation is to eternal glory. You are called to a place where only the "spotless" may enter (Rv 14:5), hence the need to get serious about purifying self of dead weight, dross, and disorder.*

If you doubt your own goodness and potential to do great things in God's name, and if you doubt the love of your coach, the blunt edge of the saint's reproaches will knock you down and keep you down. But if you know better, then—challenge accepted! If you have fallen in behind Christ as a loyal and committed disciple, then you can absorb all of the difficulties he promises we will encounter in his train: reviling, persecution, hatred (see Mt 5:11; Jn 15:18). As St. Josemaría affirms: "once you are following the Lord with all your heart and soul, you can accept criticisms as purification, and as a goad to make you lengthen your stride."[51]

Insecure people tend to take all criticism as a form of persecution—as a threat, a personal attack—but seldom as a call to refine or amend behavior. Thus, it is St. Josemaría's priority, because he is a good father and coach, to secure his spiritual children in the love of God. And you can only find your security there in the Pauline paradox: by feeling weak and vulnerable and yet simultaneously and wholeheartedly being totally dependent on the power that comes from God (see 2 Cor 12:1–10).

If he is urgent that his children attain holiness, it is for these fruits that liberate us from insecurity, joylessness, and other impediments to our vocation in Christ: "Personal sanctity is a remedy for everything. That is why the saints have been full of peace, of fortitude, of joy, of security."[52] And this is also why the saints are said to operate according to the "instinct of the Holy Spirit"[53]:

> Only when a man is faithful to grace and decides
> to place the cross in the center of his soul, denying
> himself for the love of God, detaching himself in
> a real way from all selfishness and false human

---

51. Escrivá, *Furrow*, no. 925.
52. Escrivá, *Furrow*, no. 653.
53. A phrase used by Thomas Aquinas, *Summa Theologica* 2-1.68.2–3; Aquinas, *Summa Theolgica* 3.36.5, resp. Cited in my book *Home Again: A Prayerful Rediscovery of Your Catholic Faith* (New York: Scepter Publishers, 2020), p. 56.

security, only then—when a man lives by faith in a real way—will he receive the fullness of the great fire, the great light, the great comfort of the Holy Spirit.

It is then, too, that the soul begins to experience the peace and freedom which Christ has won for us, and which are given to us with the grace of the Holy Spirit.[54]

In the end, St. Josemaría would have us do a very evangelical thing: root our identity, our security, in being the children of God. Failure to absorb this fundamental truth will set us teetering whenever a strong wind blows, the rain falls, or the flood seeks to sweep us away. In other words, whenever adversity comes our way.

Take refuge in your divine sonship: God is your most loving Father. In this lies your security, a haven where you can drop anchor no matter what is happening on the surface of the sea of life. And you will find joy, strength, optimism: victory![55]

Secure people can absorb criticism because they know where their true dignity comes from. And (very important) they are humble enough to acknowledge that they are not yet perfect. If you are always looking to improve, you

---

54. Escrivá, *Christ Is Passing By*, no. 137.
55. Josemaría Escrivá, *The Way of the Cross* (New York: Scepter, 2004), no. 7, second point for meditation.

know improvement is impossible without challenges to your mediocrity. We can't grow without contradiction.

> Humility means looking at ourselves as we really are, honestly and without excuses. And when we realize that we are worth hardly anything, we can then open ourselves to God's greatness: it is there where our greatness lies.[56]

Few spiritual writers combine as well the complete poverty and complete unreliability of our fallen nature with the firmest hope that God uses that as the material for our holiness and salvation. Hearing Escrivá's uncompromising voice, we never feel so reduced that we don't want to rise up and clasp the Lord's outstretched hand.

> What does it matter that we stumble on the way, if we find in the pain of our fall the energy to pick ourselves up and go on with renewed vigor? Don't forget that the saint is not the person who never falls, but rather the one who never fails to get up again, humbly and with a holy stubbornness. If the book of Proverbs says that the just man falls seven times a day, who are we poor creatures, you and I, to be surprised or discouraged by our own weaknesses and falls! We will be able to keep going ahead, if only we seek our fortitude in him who says: "Come to me all you who labor and are burdened and I will give you rest." Thank you,

---

56. Escrivá, *Friends of God*, no. 96.

Lord, *quia tu es, Deus, fortitudo mea*, because you, and you alone, my God, have always been my strength, my refuge and my support.[57]

In Christian life, both must go together and never be separated: the utter poverty of self and the superabundant riches that the Lord pours into humble souls. We need to get used to that balance, which is no balance at all: it is God taking us to himself and making us into living images of his beloved Son.

As far as encouragement goes, this deserves a chapter all its own.

---

57. Escrivá, *Friends of God*, no. 131.

Seven

Even Stronger Language: The Encouragement We Need

Another fall, and what a fall! Must you give up hope? No. Humble yourself and, through Mary, your Mother, have recourse to the merciful Love of Jesus. A miserere, and lift up your heart! And now begin again.[58]

Our coach is not short on encouragement.

Allow me to talk to you bluntly. You have more than enough "reasons" to turn back, and you

58. Escrivá, *The Way*, no. 711.

lack the resolution to correspond to the grace that He grants you, since He has called you to be another Christ, *ipse Christus*!—Christ himself. You have forgotten the Lord's admonition to the Apostle: "My grace is enough for you!" which is confirmation that, if you want to, you can.[59]

Reading the entire chapter in *Furrow*, out of which we extract this point, or the section in *The Forge* tellingly entitled "You Can!" will give you more of the same type of realistic encouragement. Why we need this should be plain: Jesus calls us to a perfection which is nothing less than the perfection of God himself. Of course, our perfection is relative to who we are as creatures, that is, limited and not infinite, but it is a real share in God's perfection nonetheless.

Can anyone stay the course on the way of perfection without setbacks? Precious few can, and these are already accounted for in the pages of the New Testament: Mary, Joseph, and John the Baptist—the latter two, although not conceived without sin, were confirmed in grace for the sake of their lofty missions.

---

59. Escrivá, *Furrow*, no. 166. The entirety of this point should be read.

The rest of us, as St. John Henry Newman colorfully says, "walk to heaven backward,"[60] learning from our mistakes, correcting ourselves, and then continuing on our journey. A spirituality that fails to take this process into account is no Christian spirituality, since it lacks the practical application to lives marred by original sin. On the other hand, a "spirituality" that fails to account for the power of repentance, transformation, and growth is equally unchristian and more a product of despair. Christian life is not futility, a massive practical joke whose punchline we only discover too late after many attempts and failures at perfection.

St. Josemaría never loses sight of the fact that although we face moments of defeat, in Christ we are ultimately never defeated. No matter how low we have fallen, we are never so low that Jesus cannot, so to speak, go even lower and lift us up again. The One who mixed with sinners and gave them warm welcome shows how at ease he is dealing

---

60. John Henry Newman, "The State of Innocence," in *Parochial and Plain Sermons*, vol. 5 (London: J. G. & F. Rivington, 1842), pp. 123–124. The entire passage is worth reproducing here: "At present our moral rectitude, such as it is, is acquired by trial, by discipline: but what does this really mean? By sinning, by suffering, by correcting ourselves, by improving. We advance to the truth by experience of error; we succeed through failures. We know not how to do right except by having done wrong. We call virtue a mean—that is, as considering it to lie between things that are wrong. We know what is right, not positively, but negatively—we do not see the truth at once and make towards it, but we fall upon and try error, and find it is not the truth. We grope about by touch, not by sight, and so by a miserable experience exhaust the possible modes of acting till nought is left, but truth, remaining. Such is the process by which we succeed; we walk to heaven backward; we drive our arrows at a mark, and think him most skillful whose shortcomings are the least."

with our sickness, our corruption. There's nothing we can show him that he can't forgive and heal, nothing at which he makes a face in disgust, even as it pains his heart to see us doing sinful harm to ourselves and others.

I know of no more encouraging passage on this point from Escrivá than the following, which I use very often in giving retreats. Without unduly disparaging hagiography, nevertheless there is a tendency in written lives of the saints to make them appear practically inimitable, which vitiates one of the most vital reasons for canonization: providing an example of imitable holiness.

Listen to this:

Let's not deceive ourselves: in our life we will find vigor and victory and depression and defeat. This has always been true of the earthly pilgrimage of Christians, even of those we venerate on the altars. Don't you remember Peter, Augustine, Francis? I have never liked biographies of saints which naively—but also with a lack of sound doctrine— present their deeds as if they had been confirmed in grace from birth. No. The true life stories of Christian heroes resemble our own experience: they fought and won; they fought and lost. And then, repentant, they returned to the fray.

We should not be surprised to find ourselves defeated relatively often, usually or even always in things of little importance which we tend to take seriously. If we love God and are humble, if we persevere relentlessly in our struggle, the defeats will never be very important. There will also be abundant victories which bring joy to God's eyes. There is no such thing as failure if you act with a right intention, wanting to fulfil God's will and counting always on his grace and your own nothingness.[61]

We feel completely understood by this man, do we not? If our frequent Confessions, Holy Communions, daily prayer, and constant efforts to overcome ourselves seem to yield little over time, we might be looking at the wrong index for spiritual success. The life of the spirit does not grow quite like other areas of life. Practice often does make perfect in artistic skill and athletics. And certainly, practicing virtue does build moral strength.

But we are looking to grow the life of Christ within ourselves. In fact, we are in the process of growing more and more into the likeness of Jesus in how we think, love, and act. It is transformation on the deepest level, conformity of the most exact kind. And so all of the back-and-forth of our spiritual life, and even the repeated failures, should accomplish one very important thing: humility. Without humility as the foundation of our life in Christ, there will be no life at all. There might

---

61. Escrivá, *Christ Is Passing By*, no. 76.

be external imitation, and plenty of inspiring ideals and wishful thinking in the mind of the disciple, but until we descend into the depths of our nothingness, no edifice can rise.

The Lord, and the New Testament authors, love to quote Psalm 118:22: "The stone the builders rejected has become the cornerstone."[62] It is ironic, paradoxical, and yet the first principle of the kingdom of God: As Christ is the rejected stone that supports the entire edifice of the Church, so must we build our own spiritual life on that rejected stone—not upon our own excellence or strength, but upon the strength of the One whose lowliness and "weakness" is stronger than any greatness that is in man.

Our field of battle is also the job site where the spiritual edifice grows, and we are constantly waging war within against our tendencies to self-assertion, complacency, and egotism. The fight can potentially discourage, especially when we give ground here or there. But even here, our coach has a ready answer:

> I know that the moment we talk about fighting we recall our weakness and we foresee falls and mistakes. God takes this into account. As we walk along it is inevitable that we will raise dust; we are creatures and full of defects. I would almost say that we will always need defects. They are the

---

62. NABRE Translation.

shadow which shows up the light of God's grace and our resolve to respond to God's kindness. And this *chiaroscuro* will make us human, humble, understanding and generous.[63]

That is the point: the battle, the building, when rightly understood—the setbacks taken in stride—render us more "human, humble, understanding and generous." With those virtues well practiced, nothing can really stop us, not even our own failures, since we are referring everything to the Lord. Even our shadows cannot help but throw the light of God's grace into glorious relief!

---

63. Escrivá, *Christ Is Passing By*, no 76.

Eight

Struggle & Perseverance

We cannot take it easy. Our Lord wants us to fight more, on a broader front, more intensely each day. We have an obligation to outdo ourselves, for in this competition the only goal is to arrive at the glory of heaven. And if we did not reach heaven, the whole thing would have been useless.[64]

In literature, as in real life, conflict means a struggle between opposing forces. No conflict, no story. Try constructing a drama without an inciting incident that introduces the central conflict and you will have no drama at all, because there will be no tension, nothing that needs overcoming. As a work of literature, it will fail to be anything more than

---

64. Escrivá, *Christ is Passing By*, no. 77.

a record of fictional events, and so will fail to demonstrate a purpose or make a point.

Life can sometimes seem like that: no plot, no purpose, no resolution, nothing to make sense of it all—yet it is fraught with conflict. As Christians, we are called to engage conflict with purpose, and to keep up the fight, even in the face of apparent defeat. I say "apparent defeat" because, although sometimes we do fail and need to confess our failures, our coach denies failure for one who refuses to quit: "So you have failed? You—be convinced of it—cannot fail. You haven't failed; you have gained experience. On you go!"[65]

More than an inspirational slogan, he not only means that the struggle to overcome has value, but also that failure (rightly understood) has value as well. Call it a negative value, but in God's hands even our failures can rebound to good if we accept them with humility and contrition. We are talking here about two kinds of failure: moral failure, which means sin or at least imperfection, and the failure of our good works to produce the hoped-for fruit.

As for the latter, St. Josemaría is unambiguous:

---

65. Escrivá, *The Way*, no. 405.

You say you've failed! We never fail. You placed your confidence wholly in God. Nor did you neglect any human means.

Convince yourself of this truth: your success—this time, in this—was to fail. Give thanks to our Lord . . . and try again![66]

As to the former, moral failure, the victory envisioned is not so much ours as that of our Savior:

If, alas, one falls, one must get up at once. With God's help, which will never be lacking if the proper means are used, one must seek to arrive at repentance as quickly as possible, to be humbly sincere and to make amends so that the momentary failure is transformed into a great victory for Jesus Christ.[67]

But it is a victory that we, too, share in. Because in forgiving us our failures, we are shown that our own power to do wrong can never outweigh the sovereignty of God's mercy toward even the most foolish and faithless among us. It is the triumph of grace, restoring a man to his lost integrity, and renewing joy and hope in his soul.

St. Josemaría always has consoling alternatives to sulking and quitting:

---

66. Escrivá, *The Way*, no. 404.
67. Escrivá, *Friends of God*, no. 186.

As we call to mind our infidelities, and so many mistakes, weaknesses, so much cowardice—each one of us has his own experience—let us repeat to Our Lord, from the bottom of our hearts, Peter's cry of contrition, *Domine, tu omnia nosti, tu scis quia amo te!* "Lord, you know all things, you know that I love you, despite my wretchedness!" And I would even add, "You know that I love you, precisely because of my wretchedness, for it leads me to rely on you who are my strength: *quia tu es, Deus, fortitudo mea*." And at that point let us start again.[68]

The problem we face is to tire of restarting our engine once it has died for the umpteenth time. The temptation to back out of the conflict, the struggle, that meets us each day, makes us say, "I'm tired of fighting," or, "I'm tired of feeling the tension between good and evil in my heart and the strain in my bodily members." St. Paul's "war" is every man's war: "I see in my members another law at war with the law of my mind and making me captive to the law of sin which dwells in my members" (Rom 7:23).

No one disputes the unpleasantness of all this. God told Job to expect it from birth: "[M]an is born to trouble as the sparks fly upward" (Jb 5:7). But expected or not, accepted heartily or endured faintheartedly, we are back at needing a purpose, a meaning, to motivate us never to surrender.

Let me squeeze in one further point before locating that purpose. To up the ante a little, we might complain that our daily struggles are so remedial that they don't even approach those of the saints. We struggle daily not only to become holy, but just to be good people—naturally good, naturally virtuous. The daily test of basic virtues like patience, kindness, honesty, and the like is often more than enough to engage us, let alone the heroic virtues of the saints. This fact alone can make the struggle seem so rudimentary as to be useless, as though we are always recovering lost ground instead of moving forward.

But let me pitch a crazy solution, echoing both St. Paul and St. Josemaría[69]: if we spend years contending with our faults without apparently getting anywhere, it might be that God has left them there precisely to trouble us. Why? Because there's nothing like a persistent fault to grab the attention of the soul striving for holiness. The slothful shrug off their failures and fall back to sleep. The zealous feel their inconsistency and burn to overcome. The disturbance should inspire soul-searching, a getting to the root of the problem. And this is why God negotiates our spiritual progress with the coinage of failure.

---

69. See 2 Cor 12:1–10; Escrivá, *Christ Is Passing By*, no. 76.

Our surface disturbances (temptations, passions, impulses) should lead us inward to reflect on their underlying causes. Obviously, the effects of original sin are still with us, leaving behind what St Thomas Aquinas calls *fomes peccati*, normally translated as "tinder" or "kindling material" for sin. The *Catechism* expands on this rudimentary fact:

> Yet certain temporal consequences of sin remain in the baptized, such as suffering, illness, death, and such frailties inherent in life as weaknesses of character, and so on, as well as an inclination to sin that Tradition calls *concupiscence*, or metaphorically, "the tinder for sin" (*fomes peccati*); since concupiscence "is left for us to wrestle with, it cannot harm those who do not consent but manfully resist it by the grace of Jesus Christ." Indeed, "an athlete is not crowned unless he competes according to the rules."[70]

Our coach cautions us against feeling surprise over these unruly inclinations that come and go for reasons we do not often understand.

> Don't be ashamed to discover in your heart the *fomes peccati*—the inclination to evil, which will be with you as long as you live, for nobody is free from this burden.

---

70. *Catechism of the Catholic Church*, 2nd ed. (Washington, D.C.: Libreria Editrice Vaticana–United States Conference of Catholic Bishops, 2000), no. 1264.

> Don't be ashamed, because the all-powerful and merciful Lord has given us all the means we need for overcoming this inclination: the sacraments, a life of piety and sanctified work.
>
> Persevere in using these means, ever ready to begin again and again without getting discouraged.[71]

As the *Catechism* acknowledges a lifelong wrestling match within ourselves, and as St. Josemaría calmly urges us to continue on with the ordinary means of fighting, we are still left with an unpleasant tension. We would rather have total peace in mind and body, a heart not restless, no battles to fight. And yet since God does nothing nor allows anything in vain, a great spiritual good can be had from the struggle.

What makes our habitual sins flare up from this burnable stubble, what makes them repeat and creates the habit, is what the Lord calls us to examine. Taking a step back from the sin, we should ask ourselves: *What is my root sickness? How does this personal issue open me to hear the gospel? How does this open me to receive grace? How does this affliction touch me where I hurt most? How does this or that problem make me feel so inadequate that I feel the need for Jesus?*

---

71. Escrivá, *The Forge*, no. 119.

We really can't get to the root of our faults without honest reflection before God, and then sincere prayer that he eradicate what is displeasing to him. Employing gospel imagery, our coach exhorts both vigilance and merciless uprooting of the weeds (tares) sown by sin in our lives, while also acknowledging the discomfort of a gaping "wound" left by the torn out weed:

> Uproot them once and for all! God's grace is enough for you. Do not be afraid of leaving an empty space, a wound. The Lord will plant new seed of his there: love of God, fraternal charity, apostolic zeal. And after a certain time not the slightest sign will remain of those tares. That is if, while there is still time, you pull it out by the roots, and better still, if you do not fall asleep, and watch your field overnight.[72]

The fact that we cannot have absolute dominion over ourselves must direct us to the One on whose Lordship we must lean, to whom we must surrender. And, in a profound sense, submitting to the healing touch of our Physician, learning to surrender because we cannot stand on our own, nor overcome adversity on our own, is not just "smart" Christian living. It is the key to intimacy with Christ.

---

72. Escrivá, *Furrow*, no. 677.

We should let Jesus know that we are children. And when children are tiny and innocent, what a lot of effort it takes for them to go up one step. They look as though they are wasting their time, but eventually they manage to climb up. Now there is another step. Crawling on their hands and knees, and putting their whole body into it, they score another success—one more step. Then they start again. What an effort! There are only a few more steps to go now. But then the toddler stumbles, and—whoops!—down he goes. With bumps all over and in floods of tears, the poor child sets out and begins to try again.

We are just like that, Jesus, when we are on our own. Please take us up in your loving arms, like a big and good Friend of the simple child. Do not leave us until we have reached the top. And then—oh then!—we will know how to correspond to your Merciful Love, with the daring of young children, telling you, sweet Lord, that after Mary and Joseph, there never has been nor will there ever be a mortal soul—and there have been some who have been really crazy—who loves you as much as I love you.[73]

You see how the sickness of self-reliance is healed by the humility of dependence—and not just the dependence of one who goes to another out of practical necessity (a

---

73. Escrivá, *The Forge*, no. 346.

tax agent, an auto mechanic, etc.), but out of a genuine "organic" need. Jesus completes us, fills our emptiness, and is the strength for which our weakness exists. Once we get this, we are so overwhelmed by his love that we end up saying such crazy things to him as our coach suggests.

That I could love God in a way second only to Mary and Joseph? I do believe that's what the man said. School's in session here: our pusillanimity is exposed by the teacher's magnanimity; we are mere rookies to his expertise. St. Josemaría knows the Lord and he knows himself. Most importantly, he knows how both kinds of knowledge mesh.

Why we need to learn this is because within each of us is a child of Adam who does not fully trust God. There is someone who wants to control his own life down to the last detail, someone who struggles to believe that God can and will meet all of his needs, someone who questions God's efficiency and foresight and his unbelievable patience—with all that's wrong in the world and in my life—and someone who absolutely dreads the full implications of the stark order: "Follow me."

The correction of this disorder explains why, as the apostles follow Jesus, he constantly does things that set them off. He lets them be frightened at sea, confused on land, and sad and distressed in his company. He does things that seem to go against common sense. And when provoked, they are very vocal about their frustration, anger, sadness, confusion. And then it gets real. Finally, the unfiltered emotion has broken through and the Physician takes it from there. Healing begins with an exposed wound.

And the healing medicine is our vulnerable reception to his loving touch. The man with the iron facade cannot receive this. The way Jesus brings healing to the disciple is to open him, day by day, to a deeper reception of that love—often through trials that make us feel confused, sad, and even angry. But this is very often the only way he can break through the rough extremes of our personalities. So that the perfection achieved by the struggling disciple bears no trace of self, no DIY holiness, but only the signature of the Son of God, which appears just below a single verse: *By the Lord has this been done, and it is wonderful in our eyes* (see Ps. 118:23)!

> Capture the flavor of those moving scenes where the Master performs works that are both divine and human, and tells us, with human and divine touches, the wonderful story of his pardon for us and his enduring Love for his children. Those foretastes of Heaven are renewed today, for the Gospel is always true: we can feel, we can sense, we can even say we touch God's protection with our own hands; a protection that grows stronger as long as we keep advancing despite our stumbles,

as long as we begin again and again, for this is
what interior life is about, living with our hope
placed in God.[74]

74. Escrivá, *Friends of God*, no. 216.

Nine

"What Are You Waiting For?"

I read a proverb which is very popular in some countries: "God owns the world, but he rents it out to the brave," and it made me think.

What are you waiting for?[75]

St. Josemaría Escrivá is an impatient man. Perhaps, if such a thing could exist, he is the patron saint of the impatient. He cannot tolerate dillydallying on the way to holiness, cowardice in the apostolate, indecisiveness in our commitment to the Lord. While he wholeheartedly respects and blesses the freedom of all Christians, he is also quick to challenge inconsistency and a lack of daring: "Why don't you give yourself to God once and for all . . . really . . . now?"[76]

75. Escrivá, *Furrow*, no. 99.
76. Escrivá, *The Way*, no. 902.

The Christian, if we define him completely, is an apostle. He is called to bear witness to Christ among his fellows, among friends and strangers alike, but without being odd in manners or speech. Being supernatural in this natural world is not the same as being odd or being a chronic misfit wherever we go. We are not of this world, but we are definitely in it, and our faith needs to transform it from within. Chesterton mentions in *The Everlasting Man* how the Incarnation is like a shock trooper's penetration into enemy territory, that the cave at Bethlehem was something akin to an outlaw's den or a dugout, from which underground the Son of God began to shake the powers of this world.[77]

That's an unorthodox and yet appealing image to the impatient and daring. *We're in! And we've got God on our side: now it's just a matter of reconquest of territory lost through sin—both people and places lost and in darkness, needing light and healing.* In this you may hear an echo of Escrivá's wish that the apostles of our time restore to the material world its original and noble meaning, "turning [all events of life] into a means and an occasion for a continuous meeting with Jesus Christ."[78]

---

77. See G.K. Chesterton, *The Everlasting Man* (London: Hodder & Stoughton, 1953), pp. 209–210.
78. Escrivá, *Passionately Loving the World*, p. 6.

An urgency marks these and other of the saint's words, to mobilize our efforts on all fronts to bring Christ to everyone, everywhere—the way some feverishly pursue merely secular ends, or materialistic and perverse goals, and with such networking and organization. This is what Christians need to do, using legitimate material means coupled with the supernatural way of prayer and sacrifice. Our "conspiracy" against the world is always an open secret, not one of deviousness and intrigue:

> A secret, an open secret: these world crises are crises of saints.
>
> God wants a handful of men "of his own" in every human activity. And then . . . "*pax Christi in regno Christi*—the peace of Christ in the kingdom of Christ."[79]

We don't hack the world to pieces from without, but transform it like leaven from within. The challenge is to be fully Christian, fully committed, and yet not appear weird or eccentric in the normal course of life. Sometimes we will stand out and need to stand out, but most of the time we need to be like candlelight among our peers: a flame small but sure, giving off light and warmth to those closest, until our flames begin to light those of others. And what happens when many flames are lit in this world

---

79. Escrivá, *The Way*, no. 301.

is a large-scale enlightening of whole populations with the truth of the Gospel. Then the *pax Christi in regno Christi* becomes a reality.

St. Josemaría sometimes alludes to the phenomenon experienced by many committed Christians in their daily lives of colleagues and acquaintances approaching them to confide, to ask advice, thereby demonstrating a surprising trust that comes from our union with Christ. In other words, Christ is attractive, and the more united to him we are, the more others will find themselves drawn, not so much to us, but to Jesus living within us.

Hence the impatience of our coach that we get going on this. These are not small matters we may take or leave. This is the Christian life fully lived. Life not fully lived is partially dead or dying. Can we settle for that? Doesn't God deserve better from us? Isn't the world in desperate need of the Gospel? If we are the salt of the earth and light of the world, we cannot at the same time rot and darken our areas of influence by refusing to exert a Christian influence.

However much our lives are "hid with Christ in God" (Col 3:3), we must possess the daring to let his light shine through the Christian character of our words and deeds:

You have to be a live ember that sets fire to whatever it touches. And, when your surroundings are incapable of catching fire, you have to raise their spiritual temperature.

If not, you are wasting time miserably, and wasting the time of those around you.[80]

The impatience, the imagery of fire, the warning about time-wasting, is all about influencing and saving souls. Christian love is impatient to do these things. And the trouble with our coach is that he leaves us without excuses. We all have ready answers for why we are not the saints we ought to be, or why our influence is not as deep and expansive as it could be. None of them are good ones:

I could behave better, show more decision and spread around more enthusiasm. . . . Why don't I?

Because—forgive my frankness—you are a buffoon. The devil knows full well that one of the worst-guarded doors of the soul is that of human foolishness: vanity. That is where he attacks with all his might: pseudo-sentimental memories, the hysterical form of a black-sheep complex, the unfounded impression of a lack of freedom. . . .

What are you waiting for in order to follow the Master's injunction: Watch and pray, for you know not the day nor the hour?[81]

---

80. Escrivá, *Furrow*, no. 194.
81. Escrivá, *Furrow*, no. 164.

Holiness and apostolate are both demanded by God, and he does not command the impossible. We might practically treat them as impossibilities because they are hard. But then, whose strength are we counting on to do these difficult things?

In athletics, it's different: it's your strength and skill versus that of an opponent. In Christian life, your strength is your weakness given over to God. Apostle after apostle, saint after saint, disciple after disciple, has needed to learn this often painful and humbling lesson, but its fruit is nothing less than *gaudium cum pace*, joy with peace, and we are finally free to be God's children:

> "I am still a poor creature," you tell me.
>
> But once, when you realized it, you felt very bad about it! Now, without getting used to it or giving in to it, you are starting to make a habit of smiling, and of beginning your fight again with growing joy.[82]

St. Josemaría reflects the priorities of a coach as he frequently, and sharply, tells his children to stop doing what is harmful to their personal and apostolic growth. I once heard a football coach say something that, on the surface, sounded like a brainless redundancy, but it is sheer simplicity: "If you want to have a winning team,

---

82. Escrivá, *Furrow*, no. 271.

you first have to stop losing games." To succeed, in other words, you first have to stop making the mistakes that are causing you to fail. You might get outplayed on a given occasion and lose, but let it not be because you made mistakes that doomed your efforts.

What are some of the self-defeating qualities we should get rid of ASAP? If we know that Jesus gave himself up for us in a complete gift of love, then our coach demands results from what we know:

> What about you, who are a disciple of Christ? You, a favored son of God; you, who have been ransomed at the price of the Cross; you too should be ready to deny yourself. No matter what situation we may find ourselves in, neither you nor I can ever allow ourselves to behave in a way that is selfish, materialistic, comfort-loving, dissipated or—forgive me if I speak too candidly—just plain stupid![83]

Sometimes we do stupid things that no serious athlete would do and no serious disciple should do. We defeat ourselves by indulging ourselves, excusing ourselves, refusing to give of ourselves.

What makes a fool a fool, or the stupid one stupid, is knowing better but not doing better. Now, knowledge does not equal virtue. We can do wrong fully aware that

---

83. Escrivá, *Friends of God*, no. 129.

we are doing wrong. But our Faith is not just any kind of knowledge or information. It is *revelation*. It is God sending a compelling message of love in the Person of his Son, whose sacrifice for us upon the Cross compels change without forcing it.

In light of that supreme sacrifice on the Cross, how can we afford to be anything other than like-minded, denying ourselves out of love for him and others? To live in contradiction to the fact of the Cross shows an insensibility to its message: new life has been purchased for us at the highest possible price. Consequences follow.

"We are not walking with Our Lord" says St. Josemaría, "unless we are spontaneously depriving ourselves of many things that our whims, vanity, pleasure or self-interest clamor for."[84] Death occurs every time we say no, not only to our sinful tendencies, but also when we curb the unruly movements of our appetites, memories, desires, and so forth.

Now, no one is attracted to a death message, unless it is ultimately a life message. Our "stupidity" lies in avoiding new life because we won't put to death the old one. And this is what earns us St. Josemaría's stinging rebuke. This is also why he goes on to insist that we must reject the exaggerated difficulties of death to self that always loom

---

84. Escrivá, *Friends of God*, no. 129.

menacingly in the imagination. Our aversion stunts our Christian lives, depriving them of their natural growth and fruit:

> Not a single day should pass that has not been seasoned with the salt and grace of mortification; and, please get rid of the idea that you would then be miserable. What a sad little happiness you will have if you don't learn to overcome yourself, if you let your passions and fancies dominate and crush you, instead of courageously taking up your cross![85]

Like many truths in the spiritual life, this one must be lived to be understood. And the fear of being miserable is one that overshadows our best intentions in cross-carrying, leaving our following hesitant and cautious. And yet, what happiness is there in leaving sacrifices undone, in going halfway in love when we could spend ourselves completely? Once we taste the fruits of new life in Christ, the old life by comparison begins to yield a flavor insipid, if not altogether bitter.

Waiting, delaying, excusing ourselves, is not what good athletes do. And no good coach would tolerate it: understand it and sympathize with it, yes, but not let us off easy to continue on a wide and easy path leading nowhere. St. Josemaría, as both good father and coach,

---

85. Escrivá, *Friends of God*, no. 129.

pushes us from behind to succeed. He shows us how close we can be to the Lord and how sweet that closeness is. He shows us how generous God is in showering us with gifts of grace and material means to advance his kingdom here and now.

What are we waiting for?

One day when you were traveling, a hearty greeting from a brother reminded you that the honest ways of the world are open to Christ. It is just a matter of launching out on them with the spirit of conquerors.

If God has created the world for his children, for them to live in and sanctify, what are you waiting for?[86]

---

86. Escrivá, *Furrow*, no. 858.